ALLAH THE  MAK

The Food We Eat

by FARAH SARDAR
illustrated by ASIYA CLARKE

THE ISLAMIC FOUNDATION

*The Islamic Foundation would like to gratefully acknowledge the efforts of
brother Anwar Cara for developing the* ALLAH THE MAKER SERIES
*concept, sister Fatima M. D'Oyen for editing, Mr. E. R. Fox for copy
editing and proofreading, and Dr. M. Manazir Ahsan and
Dr. Kidwai for their general encouragement and support.*

MUSLIM CHILDREN'S LIBRARY

THE FOOD WE EAT
Author: Farah Sardar
Illustrator: Asiya Clarke

Published by
The Islamic Foundation, Markfield Conference Centre, Ratby Lane,
Markfield, Leicester LE67 9RN, United Kingdom
Tel: (01530) 244944 Fax: (01530) 244946 E-Mail: i-foundation@islamic-foundation.org.uk

Quran House, PO Box 30611, Nairobi, Kenya

PMB 3193, Kano, Nigeria

Printed by Renault Printing Co. Ltd., Birmingham, England B44 8BS

Allah made round,
red tomatoes
and leafy lettuce

and Allah made
cool cucumbers

and hot peppers

Allah made peas in pods.

and bananas in skins

and Allah made
sour lemons

and sweet oranges

Allah made smooth cherries

and fuzzy peaches

Peaches
2lbs £1

and Allah made
crisp apples

and juicy pears

Allah made grapes in bunches

and potatoes with eyes!

Allah gave us creamy milk from cows

and sweet honey from bees

and brown eggs
from hens

and meat from sheep

But I like strawberries best of all!

Bismillah...

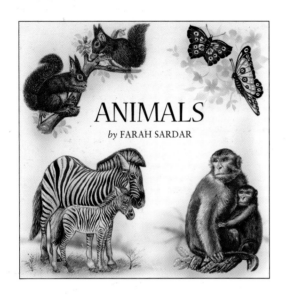

Also available in this series

ANIMALS

by FARAH SARDAR
illustrated by VINAY AHLUWALIA

An exciting and colourful introduction to the world of animals, which is a hymn in itself, bringing out in full glory the wonders of Allah's creation.

ALLAH GAVE ME TWO EYES TO SEE (*by* F. D'Oyen)

THANK YOU, O ALLAH (*compiled by* F. D'Oyen)